Around the Block

Around the Block

Poems by

Emily H. Axelrod

© 2025 Emily H. Axelrod. All rights reserved.
This material may not be reproduced in any form, published,
reprinted, recorded, performed, broadcast,
rewritten or redistributed without
the explicit permission of Emily H. Axelrod.
All such actions are strictly prohibited by law.

Cover design by Shay Culligan
Cover image by Emily H. Axelrod
Author photo by Ronald Axelrod

ISBN: 978-1-63980-787-1

Kelsay Books
502 South 1040 East, A-119
American Fork, Utah 84003
Kelsaybooks.com

Poetry is the shortest distance between two humans.
 —Lawrence Ferlinghetti

Acknowledgments

I am fortunate to be part of a small group of dedicated poets, led by internationally known poet Katia Kapovich. Every member of our group has offered insights, edits, and most importantly support and encouragement in the crafting of these poems. I am grateful to each of you.

Contents

I.

Edgewood Avenue	15
My Mother's Hands	16
Parakeet	17
Cousins	18
Tonsillectomy	20
Earth Angel	21
China Beach	22
In the Sixties	23

II.

Overheard	27
Vigil	28
Engaged	29
Around the Block	30
Wednesday Afternoons	31
Daughter	32

III.

Desert Crossing	35
Waking	36
When My Husband Goes Away III	37
Nostalgia	38
Getting to Know a Dog	39
Family Visit	40
At Home	41
Sister	42
Mosaic	43

IV.

Almost Winter	47
Holiday Season	48
Christmas Eve	49
Mistletoe	50
February	51
Flight	52
Replica	53
Neighbor	55
Possum	56

V.

On the Train	59
Eclipse	60
Old Friend	61
Questions	62
Yoga Lesson	63
Before the Rain	64
Remembering Ann	65
Sonoma Farewell	66

VI.

Canvas Bag	69
First Night Back	70
Milky Way	71
Island Home	72
Every Day at Three	73
Gilley Beach	74

Mourning   75
Collector   76

VII.

Amal   79
In Noto   80
India Dreams   81
Over North Africa   82

I.

Edgewood Avenue

The street is paved in brick,
edges rounded by passing cars
and by the rain that runs in rivulets
down the hill.
Red-leafed plum trees
line the street,
echoing the blue-red
of the bricks.

We were a sturdy gang
of boys and girls
gathering after school
to ride bikes, play hide and seek,
and climb the trees
to pluck the juicy plums.
At night we would spin the bottle
in a neighbor's garage,
giggling over awkward kisses.

When I visited in February,
so many decades later,
the street was quiet,
but the plum trees were in bloom,
soon to be laden with fruit
that will ripen in time
for a new pack of kids
to climb the trees' spreading branches,
and fill their pockets with plums.

My Mother's Hands

I studied her hands on the steering wheel,
the thin shine of weathered skin,
hands that prepared our dinner,
filed my tomboy nails,
and brushed my mane of unruly hair
one hundred strokes to make it shine.
Later those hands would pour his evening drink,
the one we all knew he should not have,
then wipe our tears when he stormed out,
leaving us wounded and confused.

Parakeet

I used to walk blocks
to buy fresh bird seed,
glistening brown husks
scooped from a wooden bin.
I changed the cage every day,
my fingers blackened with newsprint
from yesterday's headlines,
and some days I raced home from school,
the tiny bird greeting me
with phrases I taught him
in my invented bird voice.
Over time he surpassed me
in bird years, and on the day
there was no greeting
and he lay still in his cage,
I cried for the day
I brought him home from the pet store,
the small blue bird
in a tiny cardboard box.

Cousins

for Susie

In the black and white photo
our mothers hold us in their arms,
each of us in polka dot jumpers
and tiny white boots,
the mothers in full skirts
and ironed blouses,
squinting in the California sun.

Born a week apart,
we were sisters
from the beginning,
fighting over toys,
sharing friends,
and adopting each other's families
as our own.

She married young,
a handsome man on a Harley
who took her to the mountains
where they had a Samoyed named Pablo
and a view of snow-capped peaks.

I stumbled into a career
and dated a few wrong men
wishing I were married too,
living a romantic life
with a dangerous man.

Today we are sisters still,
our lives more past than future,
differences erased by time.
We look forward together,
she in those same mountains,
me in the city,
two lives lived at a distance,
always entwined.

Tonsillectomy

I stood at the foot of the metal bed,
inconsolable at my parents' departure
while my cousins delighted in the coloring books
offered by the nuns at St. Mary's,
where we had gone to have our tonsils out.

In the operating room
a gold watch dangled
from the nurse's breast,
and swung back and forth
as she leaned over me,
pressing the ether mask
against my nose and mouth.

When I woke
there was blood on my pillow
and a nurse bringing vanilla ice cream.
Soon my parents arrived
with a soft white teddy bear,
a reward for my bravery.

Last night I woke
fighting the black mask
pressed against my face,
and remembering
the smell of ether,
the gold watch ticking
across the years.

Earth Angel

We gathered on summer evenings,
the girls huddling on one side of the room,
the boys on the other, until music
drew us to the dance floor.
Parents appeared from time to time
to offer soft drinks and remind us
we were being chaperoned.
We saved "Earth Angel" for the last dance,
the one we waited for all evening,
swaying close to each other,
our bodies alive with new, illicit sensations
while The Penguins crooned our deepest wish,
Will you be mine?

China Beach

Inside the wave
the horizon ricochets
like a pinball,
and my eyes burn
in the cold salt water.
I thrash uselessly
tasting bitter brine,
scraped skin stinging
when I am returned
to the cold Pacific sand.
My friends on the beach
hardly notice,
oiling each other's backs
with cocoa butter,
and adjusting transistor radios,
newly aware of their curvaceous bodies
and the power they wield
as they gossip together,
pretending to ignore
the eager boys nearby.

In the Sixties

We broke all the rules
knowing we would
change the world,
marching to protest
a useless war,
mini-skirts dangerously short,
sweet smoke at concerts,
and the bearded boys
we brought home
to our bewildered parents.

Now others break the rules
running roughshod
over hallowed ground,
while we watch from afar,
weary of the public realm,
its endless battles
and fruitless calls for justice,
surrendering instead to the moment
and the light that falls silently
across a winter afternoon.

II.

Overheard

They sat together on the couch,
his head in her lap
as she stroked his hair
and murmured reassurance,
not ready to say goodbye.

I paused outside my parents' door
remembering their wartime courtship,
hurried wedding on army leave,
shock of families, war's end,
a new home, and darker secrets.

I stood awash in childhood memories,
of gin-fueled rages
that flowed like quicksilver
over clinking ice in the cut glass tumbler.
Morning coffee, brew of remorse,
balm of forgiveness.

Standing there I understood
what I could not see as a child,
listening to their quarrels
and tasting the fear of loss.
So I paused a moment longer
savoring their tenderness
before retreating silently,
not wanting to be discovered.

Vigil

She wasn't afraid to die, she said,
but didn't want to be alone.
So we sat with her day and night,
until her last breath came.

It seemed a small thing,
keeping her company,
so simple to sit and hold her hand,
hoping she knew we were there.

We didn't know then
that with the vigil came
all the questions that
have no answers,
and when she breathed her last,
we wondered where she had gone.

Engaged

for Jeff and Melissa

I see the North Star
outside the airplane window,
tiny waypoint glittering
in a vast sky.
He visited last night
to speak of his love for her
and the future they dream together.
How eagerly we join their dreams,
poised between a boundless future
and the memory of love unblemished.

Around the Block

for Noah

We walk around the block,
your small hand in mine,
checking for the owl
who has long resided
in the broken tree,
and for the birdbath
that stands full of yesterday's rain,
a puffed-up robin splashing
in the stone basin.
A stream of bikers rides by
to your delight, and finally
you sit triumphant
on a steam roller
workers have left for the day.
These were ordinary things
before you made them new.

Wednesday Afternoons

for Winnie

Childrens' paintings hang
from a clothesline
near the washup sinks,
while my granddaughter ponders a puzzle
then fits the pieces neatly together.

She lifts her eyes for approval,
then a shy smile, a hug of my knees,
and the trip home filled with news
of the cartwheel she practiced
on the playground.

Back home the smell of thawing ground
hints at spring's extravagance,
new beginnings, simple joys,
a perfect cartwheel,
a different kind of spring.

Daughter

for Melissa

I drank rosé with my daughter
on a windy evening in May.
We shivered at outdoor tables,
moving close to the heat lamps
and laughing at our absurdity.
She spoke of her children
with the tenderness of motherhood.
I thought of the mismatched socks
and the red-rimmed glasses
she chose when she was eight.
We drank our wine together
as if the years were merely prelude
to this moment.

III.

Desert Crossing

for Ron

We drove toward
a night-black sky,
you and I,
crossing the desert
with mesquite,
tumbleweed and sage,
tawny grasses
bent to the ground.
When snowflakes appeared,
they splattered the windshield,
falling fat and wet
in icy trickles.
It was just us,
caught in a desert squall
with an occasional truck
hauling nameless cargo
across the high plain.
When we reached Las Cruces
we traded lightning
flashing on the horizon
for the sound of rain
on the roof of a roadside motel.

Waking

I thought I heard rain in the night,
but it was only your apnea machine,
reminding us we are old.
In the morning my bones
hold the imprint of years
that have converged,
speaking to me
of what has gone before.
Affections run deep,
yet my heart grieves
for all that is lost, and sometimes
for what will never be.

When My Husband Goes Away III

Our bed is mine
for a time,
its expanse littered
with books and tissues,
old *New Yorkers* and
my phone set on
do-not-disturb.
I like it at first,
the quiet,
the cool emptiness
and solitude,
but I wonder
how I would
measure the days
without your breath,
your touch,
and the window
one-third open,
the way you raise it
every night
when you come to bed.

Nostalgia

The boxes are heavy and misshapen,
bulging with their dusty freight,
imprint of a small hand in plaster,
a valentine on faded paper lace,
Be Mine in proud beginner script.
Digging deeper I find bright bits of fabric
on stick figures, a lumpen clay rabbit
with black glaze and two blue eyes.
I thought I was ready to let go,
to emerge weightless and unencumbered,
but in the end I replace the dusty valentine
and the clumsy bunny in their box.
Self-portraits with eyes askew
and mouths fixed in crayon smiles
smile back at me as I close the brittle flaps.

Getting to Know a Dog

I didn't want a dog,
not really, but you,
it was all you yearned for.
So now I love a shaggy pup
who brings us gifts
of chewed slippers,
shredded tissues,
and sunglasses gently gnawed.
I have succumbed to
the pleasure of
each faithful greeting
and the sound of
contented sighs
as he lies between us
on the old couch.

Family Visit

When they left
the silence enfolded me,
soothing the jumble of feelings
awakened in a house
filled with people I love.

Alone, I tidied the house,
each book dusted
and replaced on the shelf,
a reordering of intentions,
a bow to possibility.

At Home

Our friends no longer
drive at night,
and hold handrails
going down the stairs.
Some are considering
leaving their homes
to live in places
with more help. Our bodies,
with their various complaints,
suggest our friends are right,
this new caution,
the need for sensible plans.

We ponder our choices
knowing it is only chance
that has placed this day before us,
its bright winter light
clear and inviting.
But what of the soft light
in the kitchen in late afternoon,
the trees we planted years ago
just outside the window,
and the slant of the crooked stairs,
angled by a hundred years of steps?

Sister

for Nancy

We know things no one else knows
about growing up in a household
full of love and confusion,
our parents' whirlwind romance
and their wartime wedding
in Army uniforms.
I was there when you cried
endless tears going to school,
and only you knew my love
for the boy down the street
who carved our initials
in the old acacia,
"EA & EH," forever in love.

Our past is beginning to fade
from your memory,
and there is no one left
to remember with me
the nights we huddled at
the top of the stairs
listening to the adults below.
Our memories bound us
in a pod all our own,
that has begun a slow unraveling,
so let me remember for you,
the two of us in matching pinafores,
holding hands on the backyard terrace,
smiling into the camera.

Mosaic

I come from the brown hills of California,
from the tarweed stuck to a horse's mane,
its smell of heat and pitch,
from the steep hills
of San Francisco and the
churning Bay beyond,
and from clear Atlantic waters
pebbled with purple shards of mussel shell,
and the gleaming black ice of New England winter.
These are the places that wrap me
in a cape of nostalgia,
each thread redolent with memory.

IV.

Almost Winter

A thin layer of ice
sits atop the bird bath,
sealing its murky water though
the birds have long since flown
to warmer climes.
The trees are almost bare,
readying themselves for
the months of darkness
and frigid temperatures
that were once as faithful
as the turning tide.
Now we find tepid days
with forecasts of snow
that seldom falls,
and somewhere far away
towering glaciers
run in torrents
into a rising sea.

Holiday Season

I string lights around the house,
along the mantle,
around the potted fern,
across the sideboard,
chasing away winter gloom
and the ghosts that appear
so reliably at this time of year.
Gin-soaked departures
from the holiday table
all those years ago,
expectations that each year
would be different
when it never was,
and now a husband
whose spirits sink
with the approaching darkness.
So in this season the house is alight,
dark corners banished
along with their memories,
and short days tempered
by wreaths of light,
a fragile bulwark
against winter's long shadows.

Christmas Eve

for David

We stand in the old church
where garlands and lighted candles
wreathe the smooth columns,
flames flickering in winter drafts.

Once, when childish fervor
sent me to church on Sundays,
I studied the bible
and posted icons in my room,
knowing I had found God.

Now it is only beauty that draws me,
and the warmth of your shoulder
next to mine. You know the words,
yet I barely hear them,
listening only to the sound
of your voice on Christmas Eve.

Mistletoe

On New Year's Eve
we hung mistletoe, drank champagne,
and wore glittery dresses
that caught the light on the dance floor.
We exchanged eager kisses
at the stroke of midnight,
and toasted a New Year
full of promise.

This year we raise a glass
to uncertain dreams
and greet the new year tentatively,
knowing our time is short.
We bow to the losses
that are likely to come,
and raise a glass to
our slim portion of chance,
hoping it will see us through
another year.

February

The barren ground has hardened
beneath a coat of rime,
the sound of planes in flight
crackles through the frigid air,
and even the backyard squirrels
have slowed in winter's hold.

We fold into ourselves,
the house an isle of solitude
in the midst of urban bustle,
as familiar ruminations arise,
emboldened by winter's capacious afternoons.

This year they are almost welcome,
those fearsome thoughts,
as I meet them with the grit born of years,
so many now behind me,
and the ones that remain becoming sweeter
with each approaching spring.

Flight

Two Canada Geese flew before me
against a dark and blustery sky,
late arrivals to a forgotten stretch
of riverbank where they gather,
uprooting the grass in search of grubs
and fouling the ground
meant for Sunday picnics.
Frustrated groundskeepers
try in vain to chase them away,
until, at some secret signal,
they take to the air,
shining black necks extended,
feet tucked against
their smooth feathered breasts,
skimming the water's surface
and gliding down the river
in perfect formation.

Replica

The couple next door
argues late into the night,
their voices shrill with anger
and thwarted dreams.

The back door slams
as he storms out
offering a departing salvo,
or sometimes an ultimatum
before disappearing into the dark.

I used to expect that one would leave,
exhausted by this sad dance
of bitterness and regret,
but it continues year after year,
its delicate choreography
now second nature.

Yesterday, he tells me,
with tears in his eyes,
that his wife's wedding ring,
golden treasure from early years,
had been stolen
from a dusty bureau drawer.

He has ordered a replica,
miraculously, he muses,
from the same goldsmith
who remembered the young couple
betrothed in Florence,
the city that held their dreams.

Now they wait
with sweet anticipation
for the arrival of the gold ring,
nostalgic about their early years,
a newfound tenderness
almost like renewing their vows.

Neighbor

We saved the irate notes
he left under our door
listing imaginary transgressions.
Trodden plants lie broken
where he used to walk
his gray-muzzled beagle,
uninvited, across our yard.
Yet when my neighbor died,
he left a void.
His dented red Toyota
now sits rusting in front of his house,
and overgrown branches engulf
the path to his door.
Every morning his wife
walks the old dog,
dodging ice on winter sidewalks.

Possum

The wreckage of winter
lay around me in the garden,
the litter of dead leaves holding
faded color as if they had just fallen,
but the musk of decay
and the nubs of new growth
revealed the season.

An opossum crossing the yard
thought she too was alone,
this primitive nocturnal beast
bleary-eyed from her night of foraging,
pointed face and pink nose
twitching as she caught my scent
but still holding her ground.

I startled at this apparition,
but who was I to question her,
a mother trying to provide
for the four small kits
whose yellow eyes peered at me
from the safe perch
of her bony spine.

V.

On the Train

On the train a couple
reads the same newspaper,
leaning into each other,
murmuring quietly and laughing
as they turn the page.
Across the aisle I imagine their life,
filled with shared intimacies,
trips to exotic places,
spontaneous afternoons
in a bedroom filled with light.
Knowing life is never what we expect,
I enjoy the fantasy
as we rumble on rusted tracks
toward New York.

Eclipse

The light faded gradually
into not quite twilight
or early dawn,
as we watched together
in our paper glasses,
a group of strangers
gathered on a hill,
huddled in amazement.

As the temperature dropped
and darkness enveloped us
there was a moment of quiet,
when we imagined perhaps
the hopelessness
of life without the sun.

When the light returned
we picked up blankets
and folding chairs,
nodding at each other
for what we had shared,
preparing to resume
our separate lives.

Old Friend

for M

I loved you
even when we didn't speak,
passing each other on the road
like strangers.
I should have been able
to deflect the sharp words
aimed by the archer's bow
of your understanding,
but my anger burned white-hot.
We were only two after all,
seeking connection
in the chaotic whorl
of our imperfections,
making all the mistakes
we had hoped to avoid.

Questions

So many questions
I wanted to ask
about life without him,
whether he lives on in the house
you built together,
appearing at the table
for the evening meal,
or in the half-empty bed
you shared.
But these are not questions
one can ask quite yet,
or maybe ever.
Instead I imagine
being left to explore
the far boundaries of grief
with friends who care,
but can never begin
to understand.

Yoga Lesson

Tall arched windows
filter the winter light
as we move the furniture
against the walls,
a writing desk stained with ink,
an antique side table,
its surface crowded with medicines.

Circle of Om, your breathing
more labored each week,
downward facing dog
now easier on your knees.
Each week a silent concession
until the day you lie on the couch
lifting a finger for each impossible pose.

Before the Rain

I wonder if it's raining in New York,
ash-black clouds gathering
as they have here,
or whether she can see
the darkening sky
from her hospice window.

When it begins to rain
I stand before
a painting of hydrangeas
on the museum wall,
falling petals glowing
in the dim light,
as beautiful in dying
as they once were in life.

Remembering Ann

The plain grey walls
and worn benches
of the old meeting house
held us in their stark beauty
as one by one we rose to speak,
illuminated by the pale winter sun.

Acts of kindness,
pathways through hard times,
irreverent laughter,
and boundless compassion,
each story a thread
in our cloth of mourning.

Unanswerable questions
hung above our gathering
like dark clouds,
the enigma of being here together
when she now belongs
forever to the past.

Sonoma Farewell

She was of this land,
the rolling hills
and dark green leaves
of valley oak,
manzanita and madrone
with smooth wood stems
the color of rust,
tarweed, lupine
and Indian paintbrush.
In the creek that once
overflowed its banks
the blue heron fishes
in drought-bound trickles,
and nearby blue-tailed skinks
push up on warm rocks
in sun-bleached soil.
This was where
she was meant to lie,
under a cloudless winter sky
in the open meadow,
one last time.

VI.

Canvas Bag

The canvas bag sits open
in the upstairs hall,
our name written
on the side
in my husband's hand.
From time to time
I toss in worn jeans,
a flannel shirt,
anticipating the trip north
still weeks away.

Soon we will lift the bag
into the car,
beginning the ritual drive,
arriving in time
to lift dustcovers from worn chairs,
stock the larder,
and clear the dregs of winter.
I will peer beneath sodden leaves
to see what spring has in store.

My bones have recorded fifty seasons,
each year the bags slightly heavier,
the weeds entwined in the planting beds
a bit more daunting.
This year I can envision a spring
when winter's leaves will remain,
soggy and wet,
obscuring the green shoots
waiting patiently to bloom.

First Night Back

There were fireworks
over the mountains
on the far shore.
From my bed I watched
the dark sky vibrate
with bright bursts,
syncopated blooms
of red, green, and white,
their pinpricks of light
arcing over the water,
reflecting the black
summer sea.
Their popping sound
punctuated the stillness
of the evening, illuminating
the mountains nearby,
their silhouette revealed
with each new display,
then slowly fading
back into the night.

Milky Way

I shed the city
like a snake sheds its skin,
wriggling free of honking horns
and jostling crowds,
the ferry carrying us
in its rocking embrace
across the water.

My island friend
in her weathered house
no longer remembers
much of what we have shared,
and rising seas have swallowed
a favorite blackberry thicket
along with the beach roses
that once lined the road.

Yet in the clear night sky,
so free of city lights,
the Milky Way is a brilliant canopy
spread across the horizon,
magnificent and unchanged.

Island Home

I stop to pinch dead blooms
from the geraniums on the porch
and check whether water is needed.
Inside a scatter of shoes ebbs and flows
as the house fills then empties again,
oars propped in the corner,
life jackets strewn on the floor.
On the painted table in the hall
a wilting bouquet drops petals
onto spent tubes of sunscreen
and beach stones once treasured,
now grey and lackluster.
The smell of salt and warm wood,
of cut grass and living soil,
the scent of time.

Every Day at Three

for the beach ladies

In late afternoon
when the sun has softened
into languid hours,
we gather one by one,
bringing news of our days.
Our bodies mirror the years
we have come together
on this small beach
at the edge of the harbor,
our bodies now stiff as we bend
toward the warm sand.
We settle into the moment,
content in the warmth
of the waning sun,
happy to be together.
Our stories weave through
the late afternoon
as we dip in and out
of icy water,
waves lapping quietly
around us.
So many summers
on this crescent of sand,
trusting each other
with losses and sorrows,
triumphs and joys,
an intimacy forged
beside seagrass, driftwood,
and the changing tide.

Gilley Beach

for Jeff

The beach was deserted
that rainy day,
its slope of egg-shaped rocks
an elongated crescent,
a scatter of shells,
crab and oyster,
clam and mussel,
cracking beneath our feet.
We unleashed the dogs
and watched them run
in and out of the water,
then along the rocky shore
and back again,
extending their bodies
in the fog-damp air.
Watching them
we caught the barest glimpse
of life unfettered,
boundless and untamed.

Mourning

Fog deadened the sound
of the bell buoy
on the day she died.
Fishing boats headed out to sea,
and the early morning songbirds
joined their daily chorus,
mourning doves adding their song.
Island life as it has always been,
my life forever changed.

Collector

for Ashley

My friend collects the sea's debris
and makes puppets as ethereal
as a cloud. Hand of lobster claw,
face of ocean-washed vertebrae,
eyes of glass tumbled by the sea,

On fine days he stands
at his easel in a neighbor's garden
painting peonies and hollyhocks
in wide brush strokes, placing paint
as thick as frosting.

In the evening we share a meal
and he recites poems
that speak of love and loneliness,
of heartbreak and of joy,
and we imagine the life he has lived
and the sorrows we cannot know.

VII.

Amal

The Bishnoi farmer's skin
is tanned the color
of the earth he tills,
his wide smile radiating the
certainty of the devout,
reverence for life,
closeness to God.

He guides us through sesame fields,
parched teepees of tawny stalks
drying in the desert sun.
He shakes a single branch
into his white tunic, smiling
as thousands of seeds tumble into its folds
like drops of golden rain.

In the family courtyard
half-clothed children
peer at us from behind a tree,
giggling at our strange appearance
as we sit in a circle on dusty charpoys
beneath sparsely branched trees.

The farmer takes his place before us,
crushing a ball of opium from his poppies
into a wooden sieve, pouring water
through the rough powder
until it drips into small bowls.
Carefully he pours the sweet elixir
into his palm, offering us each a sip
from his dry brown hands.

In Noto

The cathedral doors open unexpectedly,
the keening echoing along the ancient street.
An old man leaves the church behind a coffin,
howling in despair then collapsing
into the arms of his son.
Behind him a flock of black-clad mourners
follow the hearse, young men supporting
elders who stumble in their grief.
We watch, transfixed,
ashamed of our fascination.
Nearby families gather
around marble-topped tables,
savoring a Sunday gelato.

India Dreams

At the great fort
a gypsy family squats
at the edge of a dusty path,
mother and children dividing their coins,
the spoil of a day of begging by the gate
as tourists pass by,
barely noticing the mundane drama.

Our guide warns us
not to give them money
as they will follow us
asking over and over again.
We stop for photographs.
He lights a cigarette
and checks his cell phone.
I wish I had given them more.

Over North Africa

Somewhere below us Khartoum,
Botswana, the great Kalahari Desert,
places distant and foreign.
I yearn for home,
then close my eyes,
breathing in, breathing out.
I am at boarding school at fourteen,
crying into my pillow at night,
longing for my bedroom at home
and the smell of my mother's cooking.
I am a university student in Chicago
yearning for the dry warmth
of the California hills.
Tonight I fly toward South Africa,
thinking only of the loveliness
of the first New England snow.

About the Author

Emily Axelrod's poems draw upon her childhood in San Francisco, an abiding connection to the landscape of Northern California, and summers spent on a small island in Maine.

Around the Block is Axelrod's fourth book of poetry, following *Passerby* (Antrim Books, 2015), *North Window* (Finishing Line Press, 2020), and *By Chance* (Kelsay Books, 2023). Her poems have been published in *The Muddy River Review, The Galway Review, The Cafe Review, On the Seawall,* and elsewhere. She is a winner of the 2019 Cambridge Poetry Contest.

Axelrod's professional life was in the world of architecture and urban planning. She holds a master's degree in Urban Planning from the Harvard Graduate School of Design and is the former Director of the Rudy Bruner Award for Urban Excellence, a national award for urban placemaking. She lives and works in Cambridge, MA.

www.ingramcontent.com/pod-product-compliance
Lightning Source LLC
Chambersburg PA
CBHW030910170426
43193CB00009BA/805